For my shield this day I call:
Heaven's might,
Sun's brightness,
Moon's brightness,
Fire's glory,
Lightning's swiftness,
Wind's wildness,
Ocean's depth,
Earth's solidity,
Rock's immobility.

from "Saint Patrick's Breastplate"
translated from an Old Irish text

Saint Patrick and the Peddler

story by MARGARET HODGES

paintings by PAUL BRETT JOHNSON

ORCHARD BOOKS   NEW YORK

For storytellers
—M.H.

For Tony
—P.B.J.

1318 6430

Orchard Books, 95 Madison Avenue, New York, NY 10016

Manufactured in the United States of America.
Printed by Barton Press, Inc.
Bound by Horowitz/Rae. Book design by Mina Greenstein.
The text of this book is set in 16 point Scotch No. 2.
The illustrations are acrylic paintings
reproduced in full color.
10 9 8 7 6 5 4 3 2 1

Library of Congress Cataloging-in-Publication Data
Hodges, Margaret.
Saint Patrick and the peddler / story by Margaret Hodges ;
paintings by Paul Brett Johnson.
p.   cm. "A Richard Jackson book"—Half-title.
Summary: When a poor Irish peddler follows the instructions
given to him by Saint Patrick in a dream, his life is greatly
changed. Includes background on Saint Patrick and on the origin
of the story.
ISBN 0-531-05489-6.   ISBN 0-531-08639-9 (lib. bdg.)
1. Patrick, Saint, 373?–463?—Legends.
[1. Patrick, Saint, 373?–463? 2. Folklore—Ireland.]
I. Johnson, Paul Brett, ill.   II. Title.   PZ8.1.H69SA1   1993
398.22—dc20   [E]   92-44522

THERE WAS ONCE A POOR PEDDLER who tramped the roads of Ireland with a pack on his back, selling his wares from place to place.

He had no wife, nor horse, nor dog to keep him company, and at night he slept alone in a wee cabin on a farm near Ballymena. It was a sleepy little town in those days, but it was famous all the same, because Saint Patrick had once been a shepherd on a hillside nearby.

Poor as he was, the peddler gave a welcome to anyone who stopped at his door. "My house is yours," he would say, "and Saint Patrick himself may have lived in one no grander than mine. Who knows? He may have lived in this very cabin. Come in and warm yourself. Have a spoonful of porridge."

"Did Saint Patrick have an old porridge pot like yours?" the children would ask.

"Like as not," said the peddler. "He was only a slave in those days, do you see?"

"Did his porridge pot have letters around it like yours?" asked one little lad. "What do they say?"

"I don't know what they say, for it's all in Latin, and I've never even learned to read my own language," said the peddler. "No more could Patrick when he was brought to Ireland. They were all pagans here in those days, and no one could read but the Druids, who kept their learning secret in writing of their own, for they were magicians as well as pagan priests. It's different now. Ask your priest to teach you to read, and he will do it, Danny. He might even teach you the Latin."

"I want to read what it says on your porridge pot!" said Danny.

"No doubt you will," said the peddler.

The next year the potato crop failed, and hard times came to the peddler, for people were too poor to buy needles and pins, or thread, or clay pipes, or combs, or other bits and pieces that he sold. Often he gave away his goods in sheer despair.

"Take this needle and spool of thread," he would say to a mother. "You need them to mend your baby's blanket." To Danny he said, "Keep the pencil, and may it help you to read and write before I see you again."

Day after day, week after week, the peddler trudged about from dawn to dark without selling so much as a pin. One night he came back to his cabin, dog tired and footsore, and boiled the last of his porridge in his old iron pot. It made no more than a cupful, and he went to bed hungry.

At last he fell asleep, and as he slept, he dreamed a dream. He saw Saint Patrick standing at the cabin door. And Saint Patrick said, "Peddler! Peddler of Ballymena!"

"Aye, sir," said the peddler, still dreaming. "What do you want of me?"

The saint spoke again, and his voice came soft and gentle to the ears of the peddler as the wind blowing through the door crack. "Go to the city of Dublin and stand on the bridge that crosses the River Liffey. There you will hear what you were meant to hear."

When the peddler woke, he remembered his dream, but he said to himself, "Go to the city of Dublin! I have never been so far in all my life." That day he took to the roads on an empty stomach, walking no farther than to Ballymena, and again he sold nothing all day long.

At nightfall he had a cup of water for dinner and lay down, saying, "I'm in for a bad night. No man can sleep when he's empty as a drum."

But late at night he slept and dreamed. There was Saint Patrick again, well into the cabin this time, and his voice was like the call of a night bird. "Go to Dublin and wait on the bridge. There you will hear a good thing."

But in the morning the peddler said, "I cannot walk to Dublin. I have no more strength than will take me to Ballymena." And he tightened his belt and tramped to the town and back, not a penny the richer.

"Well, if I must starve to death, let them find me clean and decent," said the peddler, and he washed himself and lay down to rest.

Toward morning he began to dream, and he saw Saint Patrick standing beside him, shaking his staff. "Peddler of Ballymena!" he shouted, and his voice trumpeted in the ears of the peddler. "Rise from your bed and go to Dublin. Stand on the bridge that crosses the River Liffey. There you will hear what you must know."

The peddler leaped from his bed, out the door, and off down the road to Dublin.

On and on he went, mile after mile, farther than he had ever gone in his life, and then farther.

Do not ask me how he did it, but at long last he came to Dublin and saw the River Liffey, its dark shining water flowing over golden sand.

The peddler came to a halt and looked about him. People came and went on the bridge, and he stared into each face, but not a soul spoke to him. At the end of the bridge was a butcher shop with the fat butcher leaning in his doorway, his arms folded across his apron. He too looked into each face that passed, for he needed customers, but he looked in vain. Times were as hard in Dublin as at Ballymena.

The sun went up in the sky and down again. The butcher closed his shop and walked across the street.

"Good evening to you, stranger," says he. "Are you looking for someone? You've been here all day."

"I have that," says the peddler.

"And what may be your business on the bridge?"

"No business," says the peddler.

"You would be a great fool to stand here all day for no reason," says the butcher. "Out with it, man. What brought you here?"

"To tell you the truth," answered the peddler, "I dreamed three nights that Saint Patrick told me to come to Dublin and wait on the bridge over the River Liffey. He said I would hear good news."

The butcher laughed long and loud. "And how far have you come?"

"I don't know," said the peddler. "A long way."

"And all for a dream," said the butcher, shaking his head. "Let me tell you, fellow, I had a dream myself, three nights in a row. I dreamed that Saint Patrick told me to dig under an old iron pot in a poor cabin near Ballymena, where I would find a treasure. Ballymena! Nonsense! It's a week's journey. And all for a dream?"

The peddler said not a word. He turned away and started back to Ballymena. How he got there I cannot be telling you, but he lost no time.

No sooner was he home than he moved his old iron pot from the hearth and began to dig. Believe me or not, he dug up another iron pot. And when he pried up the lid, what did he find but gold, heaped up to the brim—coins and rings and cups, old enough to have been there since Saint Patrick's day, I shouldn't wonder.

While the peddler was staring at the treasure, in came Danny. "What have you got there, peddler?" he asked in amazement.

"I've got what Saint Patrick promised me," answered the peddler.

"And I have got what you promised me," said Danny. "The priest is teaching me to read and write, and he told me the meaning of the words on your iron pot. They say,

> *Here I stand, old and good,*
> *With something better under me."*

From that day on, the peddler was a rich man. He got a dog, and a horse, and a beautiful wife. What man could ask for more? He gave freely to the poor, and to the end of his life children came to sit by his hearth with the peddler's own children while he told stories about Saint Patrick. He always ended with these words: "Saint Patrick was a better man than tongue can tell. By the King that is above me, he was three times better than all I can say. And if he ever comes calling again, he'll find a hundred thousand welcomes!"

Saint Patrick (ca. A.D. 385–461)

There was a boy named Patrick, born in England so long ago that only a little is known about him. But he wrote a few things about himself, and we believe they are true. Other things we can guess from the fact that he converted all the people of Ireland to the Christian faith, so great was his goodness and charm.

Patrick said that he had grown up a careless lad, paying no heed to his book or his prayers. At sixteen he still could not read or write.

One day wild Irish raiders came across the sea to Patrick's home and captured him with many others. Unarmed and helpless, they were carried away to Ireland as slaves. Patrick was set to tending sheep for a cruel master, somewhere near Ballymena in the north of Ireland, and there he stayed for six long years. It was then that Patrick began to pray, to make up for lost time, but he thought it was too late to learn reading and writing, for who would teach a slave?

So Patrick tended his master's sheep all day on a mountainside, and slept in a sod cabin at night, dreaming that he was free. He was a great dreamer! One night he dreamed that he heard a voice saying, "Patrick! Patrick! Run away and be free. You will find a ship waiting for you."

Patrick was a brave lad, and away he went, keeping to the woods, hiding when need be, for if he was caught, his master would kill him.

At last he came to the sea and found a ship, as the voice had promised. The ship was bound for France—Gaul, as it was called in those days—a long, hard voyage, and the sailors did not want to take Patrick on board. But just as he was giving up hope and turning away, they called out, "Come along, then." And he went.

In Gaul Patrick found a monastery where he begged the monks to teach him to read and write. What joy he felt when they said it was not too late!

No sooner could he read and write than he wanted to be a monk, and then a priest, and then a bishop. No sooner was he a bishop than he dreamed again, and in his dream the voices of many children called to him, "Patrick! Come back to Ireland and teach us. We fear the Druids and their magic. Teach us how to be rid of them."

So it was that Patrick set off again for Ireland, armed only with his Bible in one hand and his staff in the other. It was the staff of a bishop, but shaped like the staff of the shepherd he once was. He took with him a few priests to speed the work, and it is said that they landed not far from Ballymena, where he had been brought as a slave years before when he was only a lad. The place is called Downpatrick to this very day.

Patrick walked the roads of Ireland with his staff and his Bible, and he talked with the High Kings of Ireland, one by one. So great was the charm and power of Patrick's voice that the High Kings turned away, one by one, from the fearsome pagan idols of the Druids.

Patrick taught the kings and their courts to read and write, and told them to show mercy to the poor and the slaves. He said that God was not cruel but cared for his people as a good shepherd cares for his sheep.

And the Irish people like to say that Patrick led all the Druids to the top of a high cliff with their devilish gods following, and all the poisonous snakes too. And there he raised his staff and gave a trumpeting shout so that they plunged into the sea and were never seen again.

The blessing of Patrick's good words and deeds fell like dew on the green fields of Ireland until all the land blessed and honored his name as patron saint of Ireland, Saint Patrick.

About This Story

When I was a student at Carnegie Library School, I read "The Pedlar of Swaffam" in Joseph Jacobs's *More English Fairy Tales*. Under his "Notes and References" Jacobs traced the sources of the stories he had collected. For this story he listed a source in which the pedlar, whose name is John Chapman, has an iron pot with a Latin inscription that he does not understand. According to Jacobs, Professor E. B. Cowell has suggested that the story was said to have happened in Swaffam because of "the effigy of the pedlar and his dog," which can still be seen in the church there. But under his "Remarks" Jacobs traces the story still farther back, to Persia, where "a young spendthrift of Bagdad is warned in a dream to repair to Cairo."

About the same time I also read "The Peddler of Ballaghadereen" in Ruth Sawyer's *The Way of the Storyteller* and liked it so much that I learned how to pronounce Ballaghadereen (no easy thing). I often told the story, especially for Saint Patrick's Day celebrations. One year, on a trip to Ireland, my husband and I drove to Ballaghadereen to ask about the peddler, but even the oldest inhabitant had never heard the story. We then went on to Ballymena because as a child I had once seen on the desk of my Irish grandfather a slip of paper with one sentence in his neat writing: "We had a farm near Ballymena."

Time rolled along, and one day an idea came into my head, a tale about Saint Patrick. I decided to include what little was known about the historic Patrick and turned to my encyclopedia, where I read that he had "worked for six years as a herdsman on the slopes of Slemish (near Ballymena, County Antrim)." Of course! It had to be so. Ballymena had been waiting for me. I moved the peddler to Ballymena and began to write *Saint Patrick and the Peddler*.